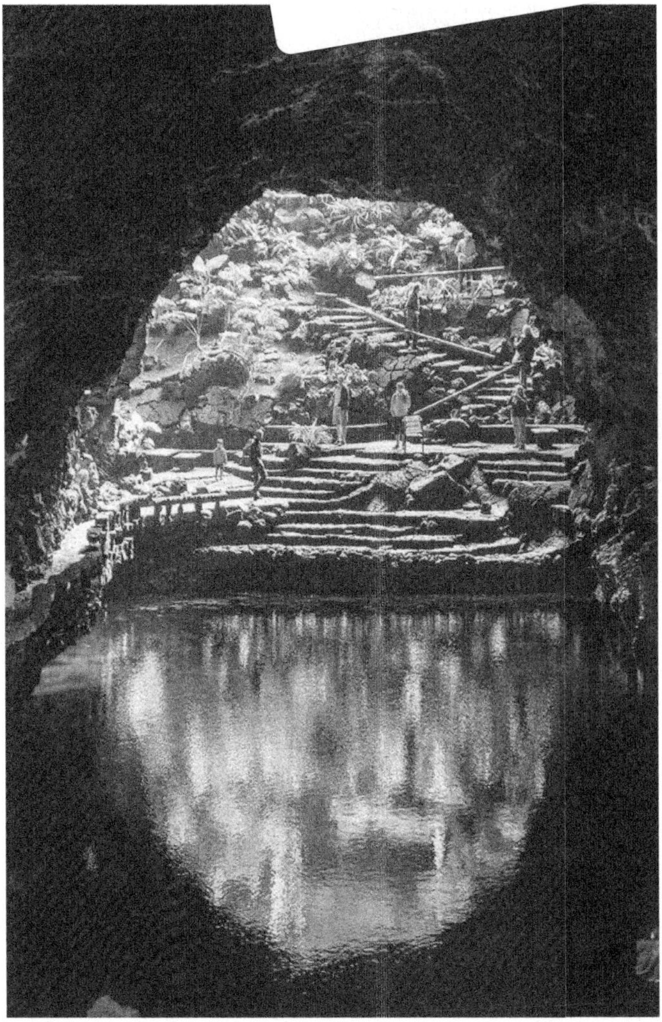

LANZAROTE TRAVEL GUIDE

2024

"The complete insider to exploring Lanzarote, Spain beaches, culinary, holidays, adventure, culture and festival, top tourist attractions and hidden gems."

RICHARD SMITH

All rights reserved. No part of this publication may be reproduced, distributed, or transmitted in any form or by any means, including photocopying, recording, or other electronic or mechanical methods, without the prior written permission of the publisher, except in the case of brief quotations embodied in critical reviews and certain other noncommercial uses permitted by copyright law.

Copyright © Richard Smith, 2023.

TABLE OF CONTENTS

Introduction 5
Destination Overview 10
Planning Your Trip 15
Getting There 20
Accommodation Options 26
Exploring Lanzarote 31
Travel Updates for 2024 37
Frequently Asked Questions (FAQs) 43
Sample Itineraries 51
Additional Resources 58
Conclusion 63

Introduction

Welcome to Lanzarote, a captivating jewel in the heart of the Atlantic, where nature's artistry meets the vibrant tapestry of Spanish culture. This sun-kissed island, part of the enchanting Canary archipelago, beckons travelers with its otherworldly landscapes, offering an immersive blend of volcanic wonders, azure coastlines, and a cultural legacy that echoes through its whitewashed villages.

Lanzarote, often called the "Island of Eternal Spring," invites you to explore a terrain shaped by the fiery embrace of past volcanic eruptions. Picture moon-like landscapes adorned with dramatic craters, lunar plains, and surreal vineyards that thrive in volcanic soil. It's a harmonious dance between nature's raw power and the resilience of life, creating an environment both surreal and inspiring.

As you traverse the island, discover the genius of local artist and architect César Manrique, whose influence is woven seamlessly into Lanzarote's identity. Manrique's artistic vision has shaped the island's development, ensuring that modern structures harmonize with the natural surroundings. From mesmerizing underground caves transformed into avant-garde spaces to the iconic Jameos del Agua, where art meets nature in a subterranean oasis, Lanzarote is a canvas of artistic innovation.

Beyond the geological wonders and architectural marvels, Lanzarote unfolds a rich tapestry of Spanish traditions. Engage with the warm-hearted locals in the charming villages, where timeless customs and folk festivals come to life. Savor the flavors of Canarian cuisine, indulging in fresh seafood, succulent goat cheese, and the island's celebrated Malvasía wine, cultivated in vineyards that seem to defy the rugged landscape.

Whether you seek the thrill of windsurfing on the emerald waves of Famara, the tranquility of a secluded beach, or the joy of exploring hidden coves, Lanzarote offers an array of experiences for every traveler. Embark on a journey of contrasts, where the arid beauty of Timanfaya National Park meets the lush palms of Haría, creating a destination that is as diverse as it is alluring.

Lanzarote is more than an island; it's a symphony of contrasts, an invitation to explore the harmony of nature, culture, and adventure. So, let the whispers of the Atlantic breeze and the echoes of volcanic history guide you through a travel experience unlike any other. Welcome to

Lanzarote, where every moment is a masterpiece waiting to be discovered.

Why visit Lanzarote?

Visiting Lanzarote is an unparalleled experience that promises a rich tapestry of natural wonders, artistic ingenuity, and cultural vibrancy. Here are compelling reasons why this enchanting island deserves a place on your travel itinerary:

1. **Volcanic Landscapes:** Lanzarote's unique topography, shaped by volcanic eruptions, offers a surreal and captivating landscape. Explore the otherworldly Timanfaya National Park, where lunar-like craters, solidified lava fields, and geothermal activity create an awe-inspiring environment.

2. **Architectural Marvels:** Immerse yourself in the artistic legacy of César Manrique, whose influence is woven into the island's architecture. Visit the Jameos del Agua, a subterranean marvel, and other Manrique-designed spaces that seamlessly blend modern art with the island's natural beauty.

3. **Cultural Richness:** Lanzarote boasts a rich cultural heritage reflected in its traditional villages, lively festivals, and local customs. Engage with the warm and welcoming locals, participate in folk celebrations, and savor the flavors of Canarian cuisine, known for its fresh seafood and exquisite local wines.

4. **Endless Adventure:** Whether you're a thrill-seeker or a nature enthusiast, Lanzarote offers diverse outdoor activities. From windsurfing in the crystal-clear waters of Famara to hiking along coastal trails and exploring hidden caves, the island caters to every adventurer's desires.

5. **Sustainable Tourism:** Lanzarote is committed to sustainable tourism, focusing on preserving its natural beauty. Discover eco-friendly accommodations, explore the island on foot or by bike, and contribute to the conservation efforts that make Lanzarote a responsible and environmentally conscious destination.

6. **Mild Climate:** Enjoy the "Island of Eternal Spring" with a pleasant yearly climate. Lanzarote's mild temperatures make it an

ideal destination for those seeking sunshine and outdoor activities, regardless of season.

7. **Diverse Beaches:** Relax on Lanzarote's various beaches, ranging from golden sands to black volcanic shores. Whether you seek a bustling beach with water sports or a secluded cove for tranquility, the island offers a variety of coastal retreats.

8. **UNESCO Biosphere Reserve:** Lanzarote's commitment to sustainable development is recognized by its designation as a UNESCO Biosphere Reserve. Explore the island's unique ecosystems and contribute to preserving its natural and cultural heritage.

Lanzarote is a destination that seamlessly blends natural beauty, artistic innovation, and cultural authenticity. Whether you crave adventure, seek relaxation, or aspire to immerse yourself in a captivating blend of traditions and landscapes, Lanzarote promises an unforgettable journey.

Destination Overview

Geography and Climate

Lanzarote, a volcanic masterpiece in the Atlantic Ocean, is the easternmost of the Canary Islands. Its geography tells a tale of dramatic eruptions and subsequent transformation, shaping an otherworldly landscape that captivates every visitor. The island's iconic feature is the Timanfaya National Park, a vast expanse of volcanic terrain with craters, lava fields, and surreal rock formations. The stark beauty of this park, often likened to a lunar landscape, is a testament to the powerful forces that forged Lanzarote.

The island's coast blends contrasting elements — from the golden sands of Playa Blanca to the striking black volcanic shores in places like Playa Quemada. Lanzarote's beaches are not just places to bask in the sun but canvases reflecting the island's geological diversity.

In terms of climate, Lanzarote proudly boasts a subtropical desert climate, contributing to its reputation as the "Island of Eternal Spring." With mild temperatures year-round, ranging from 20°C (68°F) in winter to 29°C (84°F) in summer, Lanzarote is an ideal destination for those seeking sun-drenched adventures without extreme heat. Rainfall is minimal, enhancing the island's arid charm.

Cultural Highlights

Lanzarote's cultural tapestry is woven with the threads of Spanish tradition and the visionary artistry of César Manrique, a local artist and architect. Manrique's influence is ubiquitous, evident in the harmony between modern structures and the island's natural beauty.

The Jameos del Agua is one of Manrique's masterpieces, a subterranean complex formed by volcanic tubes. This unique space, blending nature and art, houses a concert hall, a pool, and a restaurant. Explore the Mirador del Rio for breathtaking panoramic views of the neighboring island of La Graciosa, or visit the Cactus Garden, an exquisite collection of cacti set against volcanic hills.

Beyond Manrique's legacy, the island's villages provide a glimpse into traditional Canarian life. Haría, known as the "Valley of a Thousand Palms," is a verdant oasis surrounded by volcanic peaks. In Teguise, the former capital, cobblestone streets lead to historic landmarks like the Santa Barbara Castle, showcasing Lanzarote's colonial past.

Festivals are an integral part of local culture, with events like Carnival and Semana Santa bringing communities together in vibrant celebrations. Traditional music, dance, and colorful processions add to the festive atmosphere, immersing visitors in the island's lively spirit.

Local Cuisine

Lanzarote's gastronomy is a delectable fusion of Spanish, African, and Latin American influences, showcasing the island's diverse culinary heritage. Fresh, locally sourced ingredients take center stage, offering a palate-pleasing journey for food enthusiasts.

Seafood lovers will delight in the abundance of Atlantic treasures, with dishes like 'Caldo de Pescado' (fish soup) and 'Papas Arrugadas' (wrinkled potatoes) served with 'Mojo,' a flavorful sauce made from garlic, paprika, and local herbs. The island's goat cheese, notably 'Queso de Cabra,' is a culinary gem with a distinctive taste.

Wine connoisseurs will find joy in Lanzarote's vineyards, where vines are cultivated in volcanic soil, protected from the wind by low walls called 'zocos.' The Malvasía grape, unique to the island, produces wines with a character as bold and distinctive as the landscape.

Local markets, such as Teguise's Sunday Market, are treasure troves of culinary delights, offering a chance to sample artisanal cheeses, olives, and traditional sweets like 'Bienmesabe.'

Unique Attractions

Lanzarote's allure extends beyond its geological and cultural wonders to include a variety of unique attractions that promise unforgettable experiences.

1. Timanfaya National Park: Explore the heart of Lanzarote's volcanic legacy, where guided tours showcase the raw power of nature. Witness demonstrations of geothermal activity, marvel at craters and absorb the surreal atmosphere of this UNESCO Biosphere Reserve.

2. Cueva de los Verdes: Venture into an underground world of lava tunnels formed by ancient eruptions. Cueva de los Verdes is a stunning natural cave system where guided tours illuminate this subterranean wonder's geological history and artistic significance.

3. La Geria Vineyards: Embark on a wine-tasting journey in the surreal landscapes of La Geria, where vines grow in volcanic craters. Visit local bodegas to savor the unique flavors of Lanzarote's wines while surrounded by breathtaking scenery.

4. Mirador del Rio: Perched on a cliff, Mirador del Rio offers panoramic views of the neighboring islands and the Atlantic. Designed by César Manrique, this viewpoint seamlessly integrates into the natural surroundings, providing a serene and awe-inspiring experience.

Lanzarote is a destination where the extraordinary becomes the norm. From its volcanic origins and artistic heritage to its culinary delights and unique attractions, the island invites travelers to embark on a journey that transcends the ordinary, promising a tapestry of experiences that linger in the heart and memory.

Planning Your Trip

Best Time to Visit

Lanzarote's appeal lies in its consistent climate, earning it the moniker "Island of Eternal Spring." Choosing the best time to visit depends on personal preferences and the type of experience you seek.

Spring (March to May): This season offers pleasant temperatures ranging from 20°C to 25°C (68°F to 77°F), making it an ideal time for outdoor activities and sightseeing. The landscape blooms with wildflowers, and the beaches are less crowded.

Summer (June to August): Expect warmer temperatures, with highs reaching around 29°C (84°F). Summer is perfect for beach lovers and water sports enthusiasts. However, it is the peak tourist season so popular attractions may be busier.

Autumn (September to November): Similar to spring, autumn boasts mild temperatures, making it another favorable period to explore the island. The sea remains warm, and there's a sense of tranquility as the summer crowds disperse.

Winter (December to February): Lanzarote's winter is mild, with temperatures ranging from 15°C to 21°C (59°F to 70°F). While it might not be as warm as the other seasons, winter is a great time for budget-conscious travelers, and the island's natural beauty still shines.

Visa and Entry Requirements

For most visitors, entering Lanzarote is a straightforward process. Suppose you are a citizen of a European Union (EU) country or the European Free Trade Association (EFTA). In that case, you only need a valid ID card or passport for stays up to 90 days. However, checking for any recent changes or updates in visa policies is essential.

If you're from a non-EU/EFTA country, you may need a Schengen visa to enter Lanzarote. Ensure your passport is valid for at least three months before departure. Check with your country's Spanish embassy or consulate for the most accurate and up-to-date visa requirements.

Currency and Banking

The official currency in Lanzarote, as in the rest of Spain, is the Euro (EUR). Banking facilities are widely available, and ATMs can be found in most towns and tourist areas. Credit cards are generally accepted in hotels, restaurants, and larger establishments. Still, carrying some cash for smaller local shops or markets is advisable.

Before traveling, inform your bank of your plans to avoid issues with using your credit or debit cards abroad. Consider carrying small cash for convenience, especially in more remote areas.

Language and Communication

The official language of Lanzarote is Spanish, and while many locals in tourist areas speak English, it's beneficial to learn a few basic Spanish phrases to enhance your travel experience. The islanders appreciate visitors making an effort to engage in their native language.

If you plan to explore less touristy areas or interact with locals in villages, having a basic understanding of Spanish can be particularly valuable. Language barriers are generally minimal in popular tourist spots. Still, a bilingual phrasebook or language app can be handy for more immersive experiences.

Health and Safety Tips

Ensuring a safe and healthy trip to Lanzarote involves a combination of preparation and awareness.

1. Travel Insurance: Before departing, secure comprehensive travel insurance that covers medical emergencies, trip cancellations, and any potential mishaps. Confirm that the insurance includes coverage for activities you plan to undertake, such as water sports or hiking.

2. Health Precautions: Lanzarote is generally safe regarding health risks. Ensure your routine vaccinations are up to date, and consider vaccinations for Hepatitis A and B. If you require prescription medication, bring an ample supply and carry a copy of your prescription.

3. Sun Protection: The sun can be intense, even in the cooler months. Pack high-SPF sunscreen, a wide-brimmed hat, and sunglasses to protect yourself from the sun's rays. Hydrate regularly, especially if engaging in outdoor activities.

4. **Water Safety:** While Lanzarote's beaches are inviting, be mindful of strong currents. Remember warning flags and signage, and only swim in designated areas. If you plan to participate in water sports, use reputable providers with proper safety measures.

5. **Emergency Numbers:** Familiarize yourself with emergency contact numbers, including the local equivalents of 112 (general emergency) and 061 (medical emergency). Know the location of the nearest medical facilities, and keep a list of essential contacts.

6. **Respect Local Customs:** Lanzarote's culture is steeped in tradition. Respect local customs, particularly in religious or cultural spaces. Dress modestly when visiting churches or festivals, and be mindful of local etiquette.

Planning ahead and staying informed set the stage for a smooth and enjoyable trip to Lanzarote. Whether exploring its volcanic landscapes, immersing yourself in local culture, or indulging in its culinary delights, Lanzarote invites you to embrace a journey of discovery and relaxation.

Getting There

Flights to Lanzarote

With its unique blend of volcanic landscapes and cultural treasures, Lanzarote is easily accessible by air. The island is served by the César Manrique-Lanzarote Airport (ACE), located just 5 kilometers southwest of Arrecife's capital. The airport connects Lanzarote to major European cities, making it a convenient destination for international travelers.

Numerous airlines operate regular flights to Lanzarote, providing a range of options to suit various budgets and travel preferences. Major carriers and low-cost airlines offer direct flights, particularly from key European cities such as London, Madrid, Berlin, and Amsterdam.

To secure the best deals, booking flights well in advance is advisable, especially during peak travel seasons. For potential cost savings, keep an eye on airline promotions and consider flying on weekdays or during off-peak hours.

Transportation within the Island

Once you've landed on the captivating shores of Lanzarote, getting around the island is a seamless and enjoyable experience. Various transportation options cater to different preferences and travel styles.

1. Rental Cars: One of the most popular and convenient ways to explore Lanzarote is by renting a car. Rental agencies are readily available at the airport, and reservations can often secure better rates. A car lets you discover the island at your own pace, allowing you to venture into off-the-beaten-path destinations and enjoy scenic drives along the coast. Be sure to obtain comprehensive insurance coverage and adhere to local driving regulations.

2. Taxis: Taxis are plentiful on the island, offering a comfortable and efficient mode of transportation. Taxis can be found at airports, major tourist areas, and towns. While taxis may be more expensive than other options, they provide a hassle-free way to reach your destination without planning.

3. Bicycles: For the more adventurous traveler, cycling is a fantastic way to explore Lanzarote. The island features well-maintained cycling paths, particularly along the coast and through picturesque villages. Many local businesses offer bicycle rentals, allowing you to enjoy the fresh air and stunning scenery while staying active.

4. Walking: Lanzarote's compact size and diverse landscapes make it an ideal destination for walking enthusiasts. Discover charming villages, hidden coves, and volcanic wonders on foot. Guided walking tours are available for those who prefer an expert's insight into the island's history and natural beauty.

Rental Car Tips

Renting a car in Lanzarote is a popular choice, providing the freedom to explore the island's diverse attractions. Here are some essential tips for a smooth rental car experience:

1. Book in Advance: To secure the best rates and ensure vehicle availability, booking your rental car in advance is advisable, especially during peak travel seasons.

2. Choose the Right Size: Consider your group's size and the terrain you plan to navigate. Compact cars are suitable for urban exploration, while larger vehicles may be preferable for families or those venturing into more rugged areas.

3. **Insurance Coverage:** Verify the insurance coverage included in your rental agreement. Additional coverage, such as collision damage waivers, can provide peace of mind during travel.

4. **Fuel Policy:** Be aware of the fuel policy of the rental company. Some agencies provide a full tank and expect the car to be returned with a full tank. In contrast, others operate on a different system.

5. **Road Conditions:** Lanzarote's roads are generally well-maintained, but some areas may have gravel or dirt roads. If you plan to explore off the beaten path, consider renting a vehicle with higher ground clearance.

6. **Parking:** Familiarize yourself with parking regulations, especially in popular tourist areas. Most towns have designated parking areas, and street parking may require payment.

7. **GPS or Navigation App:** While Lanzarote's road signage is generally clear, having a GPS device or navigation app can be helpful, especially when exploring remote locations.

Public Transportation

Lanzarote's public transportation system provides an affordable and efficient means of getting around the island. Key elements of the public transportation system include buses and taxis.

1. Buses: The island's bus network, managed by Intercity Bus Lanzarote, connects major towns, tourist areas, and attractions. Bus services are punctual and comfortable, making them a viable option for budget-conscious travelers. Timetables and route maps are available online and at bus stations.

2. Taxis: Taxis are readily available and offer a convenient option for short-distance travel or airport transfers. Taxis are metered, and rates are regulated, providing transparency for passengers. Taxis can be hailed on the street or found at designated taxi ranks.

3. Excursion Buses: For those interested in guided tours or excursions to specific attractions, excursion buses operated by local tour companies are a popular choice. These buses often include commentary in multiple languages, providing insights into the island's history and culture.

Whether you explore Lanzarote by car, bicycle, or public transportation, each option offers a unique perspective of the island's beauty. The flexibility to tailor your transportation to your preferences allows for a personalized and enriching travel experience, ensuring you make the most of your time on this captivating island.

Accommodation Options

When it comes to accommodations on the captivating island of Lanzarote, a diverse range of options caters to the preferences and budgets of every traveler. From luxurious hotels and resorts to charming vacation rentals, budget-friendly stays, and unique accommodations, Lanzarote offers many choices for a comfortable and memorable stay.

Hotels and Resorts

Lanzarote boasts an array of hotels and resorts that cater to various tastes, ranging from sleek and modern establishments to those embracing traditional Canarian architecture. Located in key tourist areas like Playa Blanca, Puerto del Carmen, and Costa Teguise, these accommodations offer proximity to beaches, restaurants, and vibrant nightlife.

Luxurious beachfront resorts provide not only comfortable rooms but also a host of amenities such as swimming pools, spa facilities, and fine dining restaurants. Many establishments embrace the island's unique aesthetic, incorporating volcanic stones and local artistry into their design.

The coastal setting often allows guests to wake up to stunning ocean views and enjoy direct access to the beach.

For those seeking an all-inclusive experience, many resorts on the island offer comprehensive packages that cover accommodations, meals, and activities. This option provides convenience and the opportunity to indulge in local and international cuisine without leaving the premises.

Vacation Rentals

Vacation rentals provide a more personalized and immersive experience for travelers who prefer a home-away-from-home atmosphere. Villas, apartments, and houses are available throughout Lanzarote, offering flexibility and a sense of independence.

In popular tourist areas and rural settings, vacation rentals range from cozy apartments for solo travelers to spacious villas suitable for families or groups of friends. Many vacation rentals have kitchens, allowing guests to prepare meals using fresh, local ingredients from nearby markets.

Staying in a vacation rental provides the opportunity to live like a local, experiencing the rhythm of daily life in Lanzarote. Guests can explore neighborhood markets, interact with locals, and enjoy privacy that may not be available in larger hotels.

Numerous online platforms connect travelers with vacation rental options, offering a range of prices and locations. It's advisable to book well in advance, especially during peak travel seasons, to secure the ideal accommodation for your stay.

Budget-Friendly Stays

Lanzarote is not only a destination for luxury seekers; it also caters to budget-conscious travelers, offering various economical accommodation options without compromising quality.

1. Hostels: Lanzarote features several hostels that provide budget-friendly dormitory or private room options. Hostels are often centrally located, making them ideal for travelers who prioritize exploration on a budget. These accommodations are popular among backpackers and solo travelers looking to meet like-minded individuals.

2. Guesthouses: Traditional guesthouses, locally known as "casas rurales," offer an authentic experience at affordable rates. These establishments are often situated in rural areas, allowing guests to connect with nature and experience the island's more serene side.

3. Budget-Friendly Hotels: Besides hostels and guesthouses, Lanzarote has budget-friendly hotels that provide comfortable accommodations without breaking the bank. These hotels may have a limited amount of amenities of luxury resorts. Still, they offer a cozy and practical base for exploring the island.

Unique Accommodations

For those seeking a truly distinctive and memorable stay, Lanzarote offers unique accommodations beyond the typical hotel or vacation rental experience.

1. Cave Houses: Embrace the island's volcanic heritage by staying in a traditional cave house. These unique accommodations, often carved into the volcanic rock, blend authenticity and comfort. Some cave houses feature modern amenities while preserving the charm of their historic architecture.

2. Eco-Friendly Retreats: Lanzarote has embraced sustainable tourism, and eco-friendly retreats are gaining popularity. Stay in accommodations that prioritize environmental conservation, with features such as solar panels, rainwater harvesting, and organic gardens.

3. Boutique Hotels: Experience personalized service and attention to detail in one of Lanzarote's boutique hotels. These smaller, independently owned establishments often boast stylish décor, unique themes, and a more intimate atmosphere.

4. Glamping: For a touch of adventure with a dose of luxury, consider glamping options on the island. Sleep under the stars in a safari tent or a geodesic dome, surrounded by nature, without sacrificing comfort.

Choosing unique accommodations in Lanzarote adds extra excitement to your journey, creating lasting memories beyond the typical tourist experience.

In conclusion, Lanzarote's accommodation options cater to a diverse range of travelers, ensuring everyone can find a place to call home on this enchanting island. Whether you seek the luxury of a resort, the independence of a vacation rental, the affordability of budget-friendly stays, or the uniqueness of a cave house or boutique hotel, Lanzarote invites you to choose the accommodation that best suits your preferences and enhances your overall travel experience.

Exploring Lanzarote

Lanzarote, a harmonious blend of surreal volcanic landscapes and vibrant cultural experiences, invites travelers to explore its diverse attractions. From must-visit landmarks to thrilling outdoor activities, rich arts and culture, and pristine beaches, Lanzarote offers a tapestry of experiences that captivates every visitor.

Must-Visit Attractions

1. Timanfaya National Park:

The crown jewel of Lanzarote's natural wonders, Timanfaya National Park is a testament to the island's volcanic origins. Visitors are treated to a surreal landscape dominated by craters, twisted lava formations, and geothermal demonstrations. A guided tour through the Martian-like terrain, often on camelback, provides a captivating insight into the forces that shaped the island.

2. Jameos del Agua:

The visionary artist César Manrique designed Jameos del Agua as a mesmerizing subterranean complex formed by a volcanic tunnel. It houses a unique concert hall, a serene pool, and an exquisite restaurant. The Jameos del Agua integrates art, nature, and architecture, creating an enchanting experience for visitors.

3. Mirador del Rio:

Perched atop the northern cliffs of Lanzarote, Mirador del Rio offers panoramic views of the neighboring island of La Graciosa and the surrounding Atlantic Ocean. Another masterpiece by César Manrique, this viewpoint showcases the artist's talent in blending architecture with the island's natural beauty. The harmonious design allows visitors to enjoy breathtaking vistas in a serene setting.

4. Cueva de los Verdes:

Explore the subterranean world of Cueva de los Verdes, a series of lava tubes formed by ancient volcanic eruptions. Guided tours lead visitors through these unique caverns, revealing the geological history and capturing the island's extraordinary natural formations.

Outdoor Activities

1. Hiking in the Fire Mountains:

Embark on a hiking adventure in the Fire Mountains (Montañas del Fuego), the heart of

Timanfaya National Park. Guided trails lead through volcanic landscapes, allowing hikers to witness the island's raw beauty up close. The challenging yet rewarding terrain provides a unique perspective on Lanzarote's geological wonders.

2. Windsurfing in Famara:

Famara's expansive beach, backed by dramatic cliffs, is a windsurfing paradise. The consistent trade winds and rolling waves make it an ideal spot for beginners and experienced windsurfers. Lessons and equipment rental are readily available, allowing visitors to harness the power of the Atlantic for an exhilarating experience.

3. Cycling through La Geria Vineyards:

Explore Lanzarote's unique viticultural landscape by cycling through the picturesque La Geria vineyards. Pedal along winding paths flanked by low volcanic walls (zocos), which protect the vines from the island's strong winds. This leisurely ride offers a scenic journey through the heart of Lanzarote's wine country.

4. Scuba Diving at Playa Chica:

Dive into the crystal-clear waters of Playa Chica, a renowned diving spot near Puerto del Carmen. Underwater caves, vibrant marine life, and unique rock formations await divers of all levels. Numerous diving centers offer courses and guided dives, allowing enthusiasts to explore the island's rich underwater ecosystem.

Arts and Culture

1. César Manrique Foundation:

Delve into the life and legacy of Lanzarote's artistic icon at the César Manrique Foundation. Housed in the artist's former residence, this museum showcases Manrique's works. It celebrates his influence on the island's cultural and architectural identity. The foundation's unique integration with the volcanic landscape adds an extra layer of intrigue.

2. Teguise Historic Quarter:

Step back in time by strolling through the historic quarter of Teguise, Lanzarote's former capital. Cobblestone streets, colonial architecture, and charming squares create an atmosphere of old-world charm. The Sunday Market in Teguise is a must-visit, offering a vibrant display of local crafts, arts, and culinary delights.

3. El Grifo Winery:

Immerse yourself in the island's winemaking heritage at El Grifo, one of Lanzarote's oldest wineries. The vineyard, set against a volcanic backdrop, produces unique wines from the island's distinctive Malvasía grape. A visit includes a winery tour, wine tasting, and a chance to appreciate the fusion of tradition and innovation.

Beaches and Water Activities

1. Playa Papagayo:

Discover the pristine beauty of Playa Papagayo, a series of idyllic beaches nestled in the south of the island. Golden sands, turquoise waters, and sheltered coves create a tranquil setting for sunbathing, swimming, and snorkeling. The unspoiled natural surroundings make Playa Papagayo a perfect escape.

2. Surfing at La Santa:

For surf enthusiasts, the rugged coastline near the village of La Santa offers challenging waves and a laid-back surf culture. Surf schools and rental shops cater to all skill levels, allowing one to ride the Atlantic swells against volcanic cliffs.

3. Kayaking in Charco del Palo:

Charco del Palo, a naturist village on the northeast coast, is an excellent starting point for kayaking adventures. Paddle along the coastline, exploring hidden caves, secluded beaches, and the striking volcanic coastline. Kayaking provides an intimate encounter with Lanzarote's marine beauty.

With its unparalleled natural wonders and rich cultural tapestry, Lanzarote invites exploration and adventure. From the captivating attractions and outdoor activities to the vibrant arts and culture scene and the serene beaches, the island unfolds a diverse and captivating landscape that beckons travelers to immerse themselves in its unique charm.

Travel Updates for 2024

As you plan your journey to the enchanting island of Lanzarote in 2024, staying informed about the latest developments, COVID-19 guidelines, transportation updates, accommodation options, and local events and festivals is essential for a seamless and enjoyable travel experience.

Latest Developments

Like the rest of the world, Lanzarote continues to evolve, offering new experiences and opportunities for travelers. Stay updated on the latest developments, such as the opening of new attractions, the launch of eco-friendly initiatives, and advancements in sustainable tourism practices.

Lanzarote is committed to preserving its natural beauty, and ongoing efforts may introduce innovative measures to minimize the environmental impact of tourism. Keep an eye on local news and travel forums for updates on conservation projects, community initiatives, and any changes to the island's infrastructure that might enhance your travel experience.

COVID-19 Guidelines

In the post-pandemic era, travel safety remains a top priority. Stay informed about COVID-19 guidelines specific to Lanzarote to ensure a smooth and secure visit. Check official government sources, including the Spanish Ministry of Health and the Canary Islands Tourism Board, for the latest information on entry requirements, health protocols, and any travel restrictions in place.

As of 2024, Lanzarote is likely to continue implementing measures to ensure the safety of both residents and visitors. This may include health screenings upon arrival, vaccination or testing requirements, and adherence to hygiene protocols in public spaces. Familiarize yourself with these guidelines well before your trip to facilitate a hassle-free entry into the destination.

Transportation Updates

Efficient transportation is crucial for exploring Lanzarote's diverse landscapes. Stay updated on transportation options, including flights, rental cars, and public transportation services.

Flights:

Monitor flight schedules and routes to Lanzarote, especially if there are new direct flights from your departure location. Changes in airline services, routes, or travel restrictions may impact your travel plans. Consider booking flexible tickets that allow adjustments in case of unforeseen changes.

Rental Cars:

Keep abreast of any updates in the rental car industry on the island. New providers, services, or changes in rental policies may influence your decision on how to explore Lanzarote. Ensure your chosen rental agency follows health and safety protocols for the well-being of travelers.

Public Transportation:

Stay informed about updates to Lanzarote's public transportation system, including bus schedules, routes, and service changes. Public transportation is a convenient and eco-friendly way to explore the island, and updates in this area can impact your travel itinerary.

Accommodation Options

Lanzarote offers various accommodations, from luxurious resorts to charming vacation rentals. Stay informed about the latest offerings and updates in the accommodation sector to tailor your stay to your preferences.

New Hotels and Resorts:

Discover any newly opened hotels or resorts that may provide unique experiences or amenities. Look for innovative concepts, eco-friendly initiatives, or special packages that align with your travel goals.

Vacation Rentals:

Stay updated on vacation rental options, especially if new properties or unique stays are available. The evolving landscape of vacation rentals may present opportunities to explore different parts of the island or indulge in distinctive accommodations.

Budget-Friendly Stays:

For budget-conscious travelers, staying informed about affordable accommodation options is crucial. Changes in pricing, new budget hotels, or special promotions can impact your decision on where to stay without compromising quality.

Unique Accommodations:

Lanzarote is known for its unique accommodations, from cave houses to boutique hotels. Stay abreast of any additions to this category, such as new glamping sites, eco-friendly retreats, or culturally immersive stays that enhance your overall travel experience.

Local Events and Festivals

Lanzarote's vibrant cultural scene comes to life through various events and festivals. Stay tuned for updates on local happenings to infuse your itinerary with the island's rich traditions.

Cultural Festivals:

Explore the island's cultural calendar for 2024 to identify any new or special festivals taking place during your visit. From traditional music and dance celebrations to local artisan markets, participating in cultural events provides a deeper connection to Lanzarote's heritage.

Sports Events:

Lanzarote hosts various sports events, including surfing competitions, marathons, and triathlons. Stay updated on the sports calendar to coincide your visit with an event that aligns with your interests.

Art Exhibitions:

Lanzarote's commitment to the arts is evident in its numerous galleries and exhibitions. Check for updates on new art installations, gallery openings, or special exhibitions featuring local and international artists.

Food and Wine Festivals:

Indulge your taste buds by staying informed about food and wine festivals on the island. These events showcase the best of Canarian cuisine and local wines, providing a delicious complement to your Lanzarote experience.

In conclusion, staying informed about the latest developments, COVID-19 guidelines, transportation updates, accommodation options, and local events and festivals is key to planning a successful trip to Lanzarote in 2024. Embrace the dynamic nature of travel by incorporating these updates into your itinerary, ensuring a seamless and enriching experience on this captivating island.

Frequently Asked Questions (FAQs)

Planning a trip to Lanzarote involves more than just selecting destinations and activities. To ensure a smooth and enjoyable experience, it's important to address common queries related to general travel information, local customs, dining, safety, and sustainable travel practices. Here's a comprehensive guide to answer frequently asked questions for travelers heading to Lanzarote.

General Travel Information

1. Do I Need a Visa to Visit Lanzarote?

Suppose you're a citizen of a European Union (EU) country or the European Free Trade Association (EFTA). In that case, you only need a valid ID card or passport for stays up to 90 days. Non-EU/EFTA citizens may need a Schengen visa. Check with your country's Spanish embassy or consulate for the latest visa requirements.

2. What is the Official Language of Lanzarote?

The official language is Spanish. While English is widely spoken in tourist areas, learning a few basic

Spanish phrases can enhance your travel experience and show respect for the local culture.

3. What Currency is Used in Lanzarote?

The official currency is the Euro (EUR). ATMs are widely available, and credit cards are generally accepted in hotels, restaurants, and larger establishments. Carrying some cash for smaller, local shops or markets is advisable.

4. Is Lanzarote Safe for Travelers?

Lanzarote is considered a safe destination for travelers. However, it's important to practice common-sense safety precautions. Avoid displaying valuables, be cautious in crowded areas, and secure your belongings. The island's low crime rate contributes to its reputation as a safe and welcoming destination.

Local Customs and Etiquette

1. What is the Tipping Culture in Lanzarote?

Tipping is appreciated but optional. In restaurants, it's customary to leave a small tip if service is not included. Rounding up the bill or leaving 5-10% is common. Tipping is also appreciated for good service in bars, taxis, and for tour guides.

2. What is the Dress Code in Lanzarote?

Lanzarote has a relaxed dress code, especially in tourist areas. Casual attire is generally acceptable in most places. If you plan to visit religious or cultural sites, it's advisable to dress modestly. Pack comfortable clothing, a hat, and sunscreen, as the sun can be strong.

3. Are There Any Local Customs I Should Be Aware Of?

Respect for local customs is important. When entering someone's home, it's customary to greet everyone individually. Politeness is highly valued, so saying "please" (por favor) and "thank you" (gracias) goes a long way. Avoid discussing sensitive topics, and be mindful of local traditions and customs.

4. Is Bargaining Common in Lanzarote?

Bargaining is rare in Lanzarote, especially in established shops and restaurants. Prices are usually fixed. However, there may be room for negotiation in local markets, particularly when buying crafts or souvenirs.

Food and Dining FAQs

1. What is Canarian Cuisine Like?

Canarian cuisine is a delightful blend of Spanish, African, and Latin American influences. Expect fresh seafood, flavorful stews, and a variety of dishes featuring local produce. Popular dishes include "Papas Arrugadas" (wrinkled potatoes), "Mojo" sauce, and the island's distinctive goat cheese, "Queso de Cabra."

2. Are Vegetarian and Vegan Options Available?

While Canarian cuisine often includes meat and seafood, vegetarian and vegan options are becoming more widely available, especially in tourist areas. Many restaurants offer plant-based alternatives, and local markets feature fresh fruits, vegetables, and artisanal products.

3. Can I Drink Tap Water in Lanzarote?

Tap water in Lanzarote is generally safe, but some visitors prefer bottled water for taste. Bottled water is widely available at supermarkets and stores if you have any concerns.

4. What Are Typical Dining Hours in Lanzarote?

Dining hours in Lanzarote are similar to those in Spain. Lunch is typically served between 1:00 PM and 3:00 PM, and dinner is served from 8:00 PM onwards. Some restaurants may have earlier or later hours, especially in tourist areas.

Safety Concerns

1. Are There Dangerous Animals or Insects in Lanzarote?

Lanzarote is free from dangerous wildlife. Insects are generally not a concern, and there are no venomous snakes or large mammals. Using sunscreen and staying hydrated is always advisable, especially when engaging in outdoor activities.

2. Are There Any Health Precautions I Should Take?

Lanzarote is generally safe in terms of health risks. Ensure routine vaccinations are up to date and consider vaccinations for Hepatitis A and B. If you require prescription medication, bring an ample supply and carry a copy of your prescription. It's also important to have comprehensive travel insurance that covers medical emergencies.

3. Is the Sun Strong in Lanzarote?

Lanzarote has a subtropical climate, and the sun can be intense, even in the cooler months. Use high-SPF sunscreen, and wear a wide-brimmed hat and sunglasses to protect yourself from the sun's rays. Stay hydrated, especially if engaging in outdoor activities.

4. What Are Emergency Numbers in Lanzarote?

In case of emergencies, dial the local equivalent of 112 for general emergencies and 061 for medical emergencies. Familiarize yourself with the location of the nearest medical facilities and keep a list of essential contacts.

Sustainable Travel Tips

1. How Can I Practice Sustainable Travel in Lanzarote?

Lanzarote is committed to sustainable tourism, and visitors can contribute to conservation efforts. Respect natural habitats, follow designated paths in protected areas, and participate in eco-friendly activities. Support local businesses, reduce plastic usage, and choose eco-friendly accommodations.

2. Are There Ecotourism Opportunities in Lanzarote?

Lanzarote offers various ecotourism opportunities, from exploring natural parks to participating in sustainable excursions. Consider joining guided tours that focus on environmental conservation and support initiatives that prioritize the preservation of the island's unique ecosystems.

3. Can I Learn About Lanzarote's Conservation Efforts?

Several organizations and visitor centers provide information about Lanzarote's conservation efforts. The César Manrique Foundation, for example, often features exhibitions and programs related to environmental conservation. Stay informed about local initiatives and learn how you can contribute to the island's sustainability.

4. How Can I Minimize My Environmental Impact While Traveling?

Minimize your environmental impact by practicing responsible tourism. Use reusable water bottles, reduce plastic waste, and dispose of litter properly. Conserve water and energy in accommodations, and choose sustainable transportation options.

Respect wildlife and natural habitats, leaving them undisturbed for future generations.

In conclusion, preparing for a trip to Lanzarote involves addressing various aspects, from general travel information to local customs, dining, safety, and sustainable travel practices. By understanding these frequently asked questions, you'll be well-equipped to navigate the island, embrace its culture, and contribute to a positive and sustainable travel experience.

Sample Itineraries

With its volcanic landscapes, pristine beaches, and vibrant culture, Lanzarote offers a diverse range of experiences for every type of traveler. Whether you're seeking a weekend getaway, a family-friendly adventure, cultural immersion, outdoor exploration, or a relaxation retreat, these sample itineraries will guide you through the best of the island's offers.

Weekend Getaway

Day 1: Arrival and Sunset in Playa Blanca

- Arrive in Lanzarote and check into a seaside hotel in Playa Blanca.
- Enjoy a leisurely afternoon stroll along the Playa Dorada beach.
- Indulge in fresh seafood at a waterfront restaurant.
- Witness a breathtaking sunset at the Marina Rubicón.

Day 2: Volcanic Wonders and Wine Tasting

- Morning visit to Timanfaya National Park to explore the Fire Mountains.
- Experience the unique geothermal demonstrations and camel rides.
- Afternoon drive to La Geria for wine tasting at local vineyards.
- Dine at a traditional Canarian restaurant in Yaiza.

Day 3: Coastal Exploration and Departure

- Explore the stunning Papagayo beaches for sunbathing and snorkeling.
- Take a boat trip or kayak excursion along the coastline.
- Conclude your weekend with a seaside lunch before heading to the airport.

Family-Friendly Adventure

Day 1: Arrival and Beach Day in Puerto del Carmen

- Arrive and settle into a family-friendly resort in Puerto del Carmen.

- Spend the day at Playa Grande, a long sandy beach with calm waters.
- Explore the lively promenade with shops and ice cream parlors.

Day 2: Rancho Texas Park and Water Activities

- Visit Rancho Texas Park for a day of animal shows and water attractions.
- Afternoon family-friendly snorkeling or paddleboarding in Playa Chica.
- Evening stroll and dinner at the Old Town Harbour.

Day 3: Submarine Safari and Playa Blanca

- Embark on a submarine safari for an underwater adventure.
- Head to Playa Blanca for a family-friendly day at the Aqualava Water Park.
- Conclude your family adventure with a seafood dinner overlooking the sea.

Cultural Immersion

Day 1: Arrival and César Manrique Tour

- Arrive and check into a boutique hotel in Arrecife.
- Explore the César Manrique Foundation and understand his impact on the island.
- Dinner in the historic center of Arrecife with local Canarian cuisine.

Day 2: Teguise Market and Jameos del Agua

- Morning visit to Teguise market for local crafts and products.
- Afternoon exploration of Jameos del Agua, César Manrique's masterpiece.
- Dinner at a traditional Canarian restaurant with live music.

Day 3: Local Artisans and Culinary Experience

- Visit local artisan workshops for pottery, weaving, and traditional crafts.
- Take a cooking class to learn about Canarian culinary traditions.
- Farewell dinner at a restaurant showcasing local dishes with a modern twist.

Outdoor Enthusiast's Itinerary

Day 1: Arrival and Hiking in the Fire Mountains

- Arrive in Lanzarote and head to a cozy guesthouse near Timanfaya.
- Afternoon hike through the otherworldly landscapes of the Fire Mountains.
- Sunset photography session capturing the unique volcanic scenery.

Day 2: Mountain Biking and Windsurfing

- Morning mountain biking adventure through La Geria's vineyards.
- Afternoon windsurfing at Famara Beach, known for its consistent waves.
- Evening beachside barbecue to recharge after an active day.

Day 3: Scuba Diving and Stargazing

- Morning scuba diving excursion in the crystal-clear waters of Playa Chica.
- Afternoon relaxation on the beaches of Papagayo.
- Evening stargazing tour to witness the clear skies and constellations.

Relaxation Retreat

Day 1: Arrival and Wellness Resort Check-In

- Arrive in Lanzarote and check into a luxury wellness resort in Costa Teguise.
- Afternoon spa treatment and relaxation by the pool.
- Sunset yoga session on the beach.

Day 2: Coastal Walk and Thalassotherapy

- Morning coastal walk along the Playa de las Cucharas.
- Afternoon thalassotherapy session at a spa with ocean views.
- Sunset meditation at a serene seaside spot.

Day 3: Sailing and Gastronomic Delights

- Daytime sailing excursion along the coast.
- Gourmet seafood lunch on the boat.
- Evening fine dining experience at a Michelin-starred restaurant.

Each sample itinerary is designed to cater to different travel preferences, ensuring a memorable and personalized experience on the captivating island of Lanzarote. Whether you seek adventure, cultural immersion, outdoor exploration, family-friendly activities, or a relaxation retreat, Lanzarote offers a diverse range of possibilities for an unforgettable getaway.

Additional Resources

As you embark on your journey to Lanzarote, accessing useful websites, apps, and contact information for local authorities is essential for a seamless and enjoyable experience. Here's a comprehensive guide to additional resources that will enhance your travel planning and ensure a smooth stay on the island.

Useful Websites and Apps

1. Tourist Board of Lanzarote:

    - The official tourist board website provides comprehensive information on attractions, activities, and events in Lanzarote. Explore travel guides, maps, and the latest updates.

2. Visit Canary Islands:

    - The official tourism website for the Canary Islands offers insights into the entire archipelago, including Lanzarote. Discover travel tips, itineraries, and cultural highlights.

3. Lanzarote Guidebook App:

    - Download the Lanzarote Guidebook app for detailed information on attractions, dining, and activities. The app works offline, making it convenient for on-the-go exploration.

4. LanzaroteON:
   - LanzaroteON is a local events and activities platform. Stay updated on cultural events, excursions, and local happenings during your visit.

5. Canary Islands Weather:
   - Check the latest weather forecasts for Lanzarote through the official website of the Spanish Meteorological Agency. Stay informed about temperature, wind conditions, and potential rainfall.

6. Spanish Red Cross First Aid App:
   - Ensure your safety with the Spanish Red Cross First Aid app. Access essential first aid information and emergency contacts in case of unforeseen circumstances.

Contact Information for Local Authorities

1. **Emergency Services:**
   - **Emergency Number (General):** 112
   - **Medical Emergency:** 061

- **Police:** 091
- **Fire Department:** 080

2. **Hospitals:**
   - **Hospital General de Lanzarote:**
     - Address: Ctra. de Arrecife a Tinajo, s/n, 35500 Arrecife, Las Palmas, Spain
     - Phone: +34 928 59 81 00

3. **Tourist Assistance:**
   - **Tourist Information Office (Arrecife):**
     - Address: Avda. Coll, 3, 35500 Arrecife, Lanzarote, Spain
     - Phone: +34 928 81 01 00

4. **Consulates:**
   - **Consulate of your Country in Las Palmas:**
     - It's advisable to note the contact information for your country's consulate in Las Palmas, Gran Canaria, for assistance during your stay.

5. **Police Stations:**
   - **National Police (Arrecife):**
     - Address: C/ Isaac Peral, 3, 35500 Arrecife, Lanzarote, Spain
     - Phone: +34 928 81 31 00
6. **Transportation Authorities:**
   - **Lanzarote Airport (AENA):**
     - Official Website
     - Phone: +34 913 21 10 00
7. **Tourism Board Contacts:**
   - **Tourist Board of Lanzarote:**
     - Contact Form
     - Phone: +34 928 811 762
8. **COVID-19 Information:**
   - **Canary Islands Health Department:**
     - Official Website: Stay informed about COVID-19 guidelines and updates specific to the Canary Islands.

Tips for Emergency Situations:

- **Know Your Location:** Always be aware of your surroundings and have the address of your accommodation readily available.

- **Communication:** If you're facing an emergency, immediately contact the appropriate emergency service. If needed, use translation apps to assist with communication.

- **Travel Insurance:** Ensure you have comprehensive travel insurance that covers medical emergencies and provides contact details for assistance.

- **Local Language:** While English is widely spoken in tourist areas, it's helpful to learn a few basic phrases in Spanish for effective communication.

By utilizing these resources, you'll confidently navigate Lanzarote, access important information, and ensure a safe and enjoyable experience on this stunning island.

Conclusion

As you embark on your journey to Lanzarote, a captivating island blending natural wonders, cultural richness, and outdoor adventures, you are poised for an experience that transcends the ordinary. Lanzarote's unique charm, shaped by its volcanic landscapes, pristine beaches, and the visionary artistry of César Manrique, invites you to explore, unwind, and immerse yourself in a tapestry of experiences.

Throughout this comprehensive guide, we have delved into the myriad facets of Lanzarote, providing you with detailed insights into its geography, climate, cultural highlights, local cuisine, and unique attractions. We've guided you through the intricacies of trip planning, from the best times to visit and visa requirements to currency, language, and health and safety tips.

You've discovered the various ways to reach Lanzarote through flights, local transportation, or rental cars. We've explored the diverse accommodation options, from hotels and resorts to vacation rentals and unique stays, ensuring that you can tailor your stay to your preferences.

The exploration of Lanzarote would only be complete with detailed insights into its must-visit attractions, outdoor activities, arts and culture, and stunning beaches. Whether you're seeking the thrill of hiking in the Fire Mountains, the serenity of Jameos del Agua, or the vibrant atmosphere of Teguise's historic quarter, Lanzarote offers an array of experiences to suit every taste.

In your journey through this guide, you've been equipped with the latest travel updates for 2024, ensuring you stay informed about developments, COVID-19 guidelines, transportation updates, accommodation options, and local events and festivals.

We've addressed frequently asked questions for those with specific queries, covering general travel information, local customs, food and dining, safety concerns, and sustainable travel tips. This information ensures that you approach your Lanzarote adventure with confidence and cultural sensitivity.

Sample itineraries have been crafted to cater to various travel preferences, offering weekend getaways, family-friendly adventures, cultural immersions, outdoor enthusiast itineraries, and relaxation retreats. These itineraries serve as a starting point, allowing you to customize your journey and make the most of your time on the island.

Finally, additional resources have been provided, including useful websites, apps, and contact information for local authorities. These resources are designed to enhance your travel planning, offer real-time information, and assist in emergencies.

In conclusion, Lanzarote beckons as a destination that seamlessly blends natural beauty with cultural richness, offering a unique and unforgettable experience. Whether you're an outdoor enthusiast, a cultural connoisseur, a family seeking adventure, or a traveler pursuing relaxation, Lanzarote unfolds its wonders to create lasting memories. Embrace the island's diversity, immerse yourself in its allure, and let the spirit of Lanzarote captivate you as you embark on this extraordinary journey.

Printed in Great Britain
by Amazon